Cleveland Browns

BY

ZACH WYNER

MEDIA ENHANCED BOOKS
AV2
BY WEIGL™
ADDED VALUE • AUDIO VISUAL

www.av2books.com

AV² provides enriched content that supplements and complements this book. Weigl's AV² books strive to create inspired learning and engage young minds in a total learning experience.

Your AV² Media Enhanced books come alive with...

Audio
Listen to sections of the book read aloud.

Key Words
Study vocabulary, and complete a matching word activity.

Video
Watch informative video clips.

Quizzes
Test your knowledge.

Go to **www.av2books.com**, and enter this book's unique code.

BOOK CODE

K 3 3 3 5 0 5

Embedded Weblinks
Gain additional information for research.

Slide Show
View images and captions, and prepare a presentation.

AV² by Weigl brings you media enhanced books that support active learning.

Try This!
Complete activities and hands-on experiments.

... and much, much more!

Published by AV² by Weigl
350 5th Avenue, 59th Floor
New York, NY 10118
Websites: www.av2books.com   www.weigl.com

Library of Congress Control Number: 2014930770

ISBN 978-1-4896-0810-9 (hardcover)
ISBN 978-1-4896-0812-3 (single-user eBook)
ISBN 978-1-4896-0813-0 (multi-user eBook)

Printed in the United States of America in Brainerd, Minnesota
2 3 4 5 6 7 8 9 0 18 17 16 15

022015
WEP050215

Project Coordinator Aaron Carr
Art Director Terry Paulhus

Photo Credits
Every reasonable effort has been made to trace ownership and to obtain permission to reprint copyright material. The publishers would be pleased to have any errors or omissions brought to their attention so that they may be corrected in subsequent printings.

Weigl acknowledges Getty Images as its primary image supplier for this title.

CONTENTS

Introduction

The name "Cleveland Browns" makes fans think of tough, traditional football. Perhaps this is because of the Browns' no-frills burnt orange helmets. Perhaps it is because between the years of 1950 and 1964, when NFL games were first regularly televised, the Browns played in nine NFL Championship Games. Perhaps it is because one of the game's fiercest and bravest players, Jim Brown, wore that burnt orange, seal brown, and white uniform, as he led the league in rushing eight times in nine years. Perhaps it has something to do with the determined Browns fans that fought to hold onto the team's name and history when their beloved franchise moved to Baltimore.

The Cleveland Browns were founded in 1945 and began playing a year later.

Whatever the reason, the Browns enjoy a powerful connection with their followers. In recent years, as the club has scraped and clawed to get a foothold in the American Football Conference (AFC) North, players and fans alike have again demonstrated their toughness, refusing to give up hope despite years of frustration.

Josh Gordon is the current starting wide receiver for the Browns. He was drafted by Cleveland in 2012.

CLEVELAND
BROWNS

Stadium FirstEnergy Stadium

Division AFC North

Head coach Mike Pettine

Location Cleveland, Ohio

NFL Championships 1950, 1954, 1955, 1964

Nicknames None

28
Playoff
Appearances

4
NFL
Championships

13
Division
Championships

History

The Cleveland Browns were **ALMOST** called the **Cleveland Panthers!**

⌐ In 2002, *Sporting News* named Jim Brown as the greatest professional football player ever.

Originally members of the All-American Football Conference (AAFC), the Cleveland Browns were a dominant force in professional football from the beginning. Coached by **hall of famer** Paul Brown, Cleveland won the championship every year of the AAFC's four-year existence. The AAFC folded in 1949, and the San Francisco 49ers, the Baltimore Colts, and the Cleveland Browns joined the National Football League (NFL). In their first NFL season, the Browns achieved a 10-2 record and defeated the Los Angeles Rams in the NFL Championship Game, 30-28. Coach Brown said it was the greatest game he ever saw

Between 1950 and 1969, the Browns played in 11 NFL Championship Games and won four of them. Their last NFL championship came in 1964 behind the play of one of the greatest running backs in NFL history, Jim Brown. A four-time **most valuable player (MVP)**, Brown led the league in rushing yards in eight of his nine NFL seasons. Following the NFL–American Football League (AFL) **merger** and a decade of average play, the Browns became contenders again in the 1980s. Behind coach Marty Schottenheimer and quarterback Bernie Kosar, they played in three AFC Championship Games in four years. Unfortunately, they suffered a pair of heartbreaking losses and missed out on the team's first trip to the **Super Bowl**.

⌐ Bernie Kosar was known for his sidearm delivery and good health. He made 105 of a possible 108 starts during his nine years in Cleveland.

The Stadium

FirstEnergy Stadium seats 73,200 fans.

When former Browns owner Art Modell moved the team to Baltimore in 1996, the city of Cleveland tore down Cleveland Municipal Stadium. Since they still had the rights to the name "Browns," Cleveland looked ahead to a time when the

⨆ Real people, not dogs, sit in the Browns' "Dawg Pound" on Sunday.

Browns would be an NFL team once again. To get ready for a new team, they built FirstEnergy Stadium.

Located on the shores of Lake Erie, FirstEnergy Stadium was constructed on the same ground as Cleveland Municipal Stadium. Built from concrete, glass, and natural stone, construction of FirstEnergy Stadium took more than two years and 6,000 truckloads of concrete. The decision to have a field of natural grass instead of synthetic **turf** required some creative engineering. In order to keep the grass from freezing over in Cleveland's frosty winter climate, the construction crew installed more than 40 miles (64 kilometers) of underground piping and nine boilers to heat the grass from below. Just like Cleveland Municipal Stadium, FirstEnergy Stadium provides bleacher seats on the east and west ends to house the famous assembly of fans known as the "Dawg Pound."

⨆ Hungry Browns' fans flock to food stands to feast on roast and corned beef sandwiches.

Where They Play

CANADA

Washington
Oregon
Montana
North Dakota
Minnesota
Lake Superior
Idaho
South Dakota
Wyoming
Wisconsin
Iowa
Nevada
Utah
Nebraska
Illinois
California
Colorado
Kansas
Missouri
UNITED STATES
Arizona
New Mexico
Oklahoma
Arkansas
Texas
Louisiana
Mississippi
Pacific Ocean

30 Washington
29
15
16
14
23
22
24
13
31
32
17
12
27

Alaska

0   500 Miles
0   500 km

Hawai'i

0   100 Miles
0   100 km

MEXICO

Gulf of Mexico

AMERICAN FOOTBALL CONFERENCE

EAST	NORTH	SOUTH	WEST
1 Gillette Stadium	★ 5 FirstEnergy Stadium	9 EverBank Field	13 Arrowhead Stadium
2 MetLife Stadium	6 Heinz Field	10 LP Field	14 Sports Authority Field at Mile High
3 Ralph Wilson Stadium	7 M&T Bank Stadium	11 Lucas Oil Stadium	15 O.co Coliseum
4 Sun Life Stadium	8 Paul Brown Stadium	12 NRG Stadium	16 Qualcomm Stadium

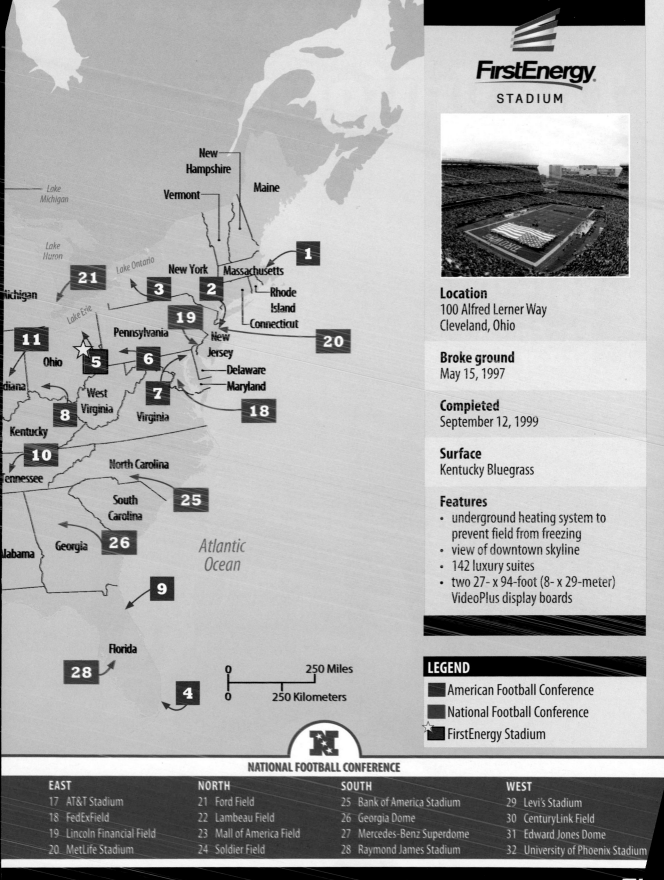

FirstEnergy
STADIUM

Location
100 Alfred Lerner Way
Cleveland, Ohio

Broke ground
May 15, 1997

Completed
September 12, 1999

Surface
Kentucky Bluegrass

Features
- underground heating system to prevent field from freezing
- view of downtown skyline
- 142 luxury suites
- two 27- x 94-foot (8- x 29-meter) VideoPlus display boards

LEGEND
- American Football Conference
- National Football Conference
- FirstEnergy Stadium

Lake Michigan
Lake Huron
Lake Ontario
Lake Erie

New Hampshire
Vermont
Maine
Massachusetts
New York
Rhode Island
Connecticut
Michigan
Pennsylvania
New Jersey
Ohio
Delaware
Maryland
Indiana
West Virginia
Virginia
Kentucky
Tennessee
North Carolina
South Carolina
Georgia
Alabama
Florida

Atlantic Ocean

0 — 250 Miles
0 — 250 Kilometers

NATIONAL FOOTBALL CONFERENCE

EAST		NORTH		SOUTH		WEST	
17	AT&T Stadium	21	Ford Field	25	Bank of America Stadium	29	Levi's Stadium
18	FedExField	22	Lambeau Field	26	Georgia Dome	30	CenturyLink Field
19	Lincoln Financial Field	23	Mall of America Field	27	Mercedes-Benz Superdome	31	Edward Jones Dome
20	MetLife Stadium	24	Soldier Field	28	Raymond James Stadium	32	University of Phoenix Stadium

The Uniforms

The Cleveland Browns have
16 **PLAYERS**
in the
**PRO FOOTBALL
HALL OF FAME.**

⊔ The Cleveland Browns
have retired five
uniform numbers. All
five of those honored
played during either the
1940s, 1950s, or 1960s.

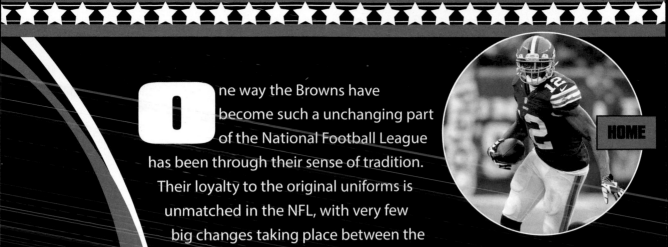

One way the Browns have become such a unchanging part of the National Football League has been through their sense of tradition. Their loyalty to the original uniforms is unmatched in the NFL, with very few big changes taking place between the beginning of the franchise and the uniform's appearance today.

HOME

The Cleveland Browns' home uniforms are "seal brown" with white numerals and white and orange stripes on their sleeves. Their away uniforms are white with brown numerals and brown and orange stripes. Their seal brown home uniforms are typically worn with white pants that have orange and brown stripes, while their white away uniforms are worn with brown pants with no stripe.

AWAY

⌐ For an October 2013 home game, the Browns paired brown pants with their brown jerseys for the first time in team history.

The Helmets

NO 'GO
The Browns' helmet is unique. It is the only one in the league without a logo.

WARNING

└ From 1957 to 1960, the Browns displayed players' numbers on their helmets.

The more things change, the more they stay the same." Whoever first said these words could not have found a better example than the Cleveland Browns. This team has adapted to different leagues, different owners, and different stadiums. From 1996 to 1998, the players had been moved to Baltimore and there was no football in Cleveland. When football returned in 1999, the Browns wore the same uniforms and the same helmets that they had since 1961.

While the Browns started out wearing the traditional leather helmets, by the 1950s, the league required players to wear plastic helmets and a facemask in order to protect from injury. Choosing a basic approach, the Browns chose not to put a **logo** on their helmet and instead wore burnt orange with a brown-white-brown stripe down the center. To this day, this original design has gone largely unchanged.

↳ Tough football is a contact sport, contact such as helmet-to-helmet hits can be flagged as unsportsmanlike and are punishable by a 15-yard penalty.

The Coaches

5 The number of years that Bill Belichick coached the Browns. The team recorded a 36-44 win-loss record during Belichick's seasons in Cleveland.

⌐ Mike Pettine was an assistant coach for three NFL teams before becoming the head man in Cleveland.

More than any other sport, professional football head coaches are thrust into the spotlight. The legacy of hall of fame coach Paul Brown has survived in the coaches who have come after him, as Cleveland coaches Blanton Collier, Forrest Gregg, and Sam Rutigliano earned Coach of the Year awards.

PAUL BROWN

Paul Brown brought the city of Cleveland three NFL Championships. A winner and an innovator, he was the first coach to use intelligence tests, scout opposing teams with game film, and was the inventor of the **draw play**.

MARTY SCHOTTENHEIMER

Totaling 44 regular-season wins, Marty Schottenheimer was the Browns' most successful head coach since Blanton Collier in the 1960s. Schottenheimer led the Browns to three straight Central Division titles and back-to-back AFC Championship Games.

MIKE PETTINE

Son of a legendary high school football coach, Mike Pettine has officially stepped out of his father's shadow. Since becoming an NFL assistant coach in 2002, he has been recognized for his work with the 2009 NY Jets league-leading defense, and for the job he did as the defensive coordinator of the 2013 Buffalo Bills. The 2014 Browns are in good hands.

The Mascot

While his favorite drink may be chocolate milk, Chomps lists his favorite foods as Roasted Raven and Baked Bengal Tiger. The Cincinnati Bengals and the Baltimore Ravens are two of the Browns' biggest rivals.

At 6 feet, 1 inch and 195 pounds, Chomps is a lean, mean, cheering machine. This brown Labrador makes his home in Cleveland's famous Dawg Pound where he has befriended legions of die-hard Browns fans throughout the years.

⌐ In 2008, Chomps traveled to Hawai'i to support the Special Olympics.

A gym rat and bookworm, Chomps loves to exercise and read during his time off, keeping both mind and body sharp in preparation for some serious cheering on Sunday afternoons. In addition to Browns games, Chomps performs at birthday parties, fundraisers, and charity events.

On September 13, 2013, the Browns' original mascot, "Brownie the Elf," came out of retirement to join Chomps on the Browns' sideline. This marked the first appearance at a Browns game for Brownie the Elf since 1969.

⌐ Chomps's favorite movies are *Beethoven*, *101 Dalmatians*, and *Dr. Dolittle*.

Legends of the Past

Many great players have suited up in the Browns' brown and orange. A few of them have become icons of the team and the city it represents.

Jim Brown

Position Fullback
Seasons 9 (1956–1965)
Born February 17, 1936, in St. Simons, Georgia

In nine NFL seasons, Jim Brown made nine **Pro Bowls**, was voted a first-team **All-Pro** eight times, and led the league in rushing eight times. His ability to catch passes out of the **backfield** made him a regular target of Browns' quarterbacks, resulting in Brown leading the league in **yards from scrimmage** six times. His career average of 104.3 rushing yards per game is the highest in NFL history. A hall of famer and four-time MVP, Jim Brown was a champion on and off the field. Since retiring, he has worked tirelessly to teach important life skills to gang members in inner cities and prisons.

Ozzie Newsome

There is no greater indicator of a player's place in history than permanent changes to the position they played. Before Ozzie Newsome, tight ends rarely lined up as receivers. This strategy changed due to Newsome's great hands and athleticism. In 13 seasons with Cleveland, Newsome set then-NFL tight end records for receptions (682), receiving yards (7,980), and touchdowns (47). Also, during his career, Newsome never missed a game, playing in 198 straight contests. In 1999, Newsome was elected to the hall of fame, and in 2002, he became the NFL's first African American **general manager**.

Position Tight End
Seasons 13 (1978–1990)
Born March 16, 1956, in Muscle Shoals, Alabama

Bill Willis

O n September 6, 1946, more than six months before Jackie Robinson broke Major League Baseball's **color barrier**, defensive guard Bill Willis and teammate Marion Motley suited up to take the field against the Miami Seahawks. They were the first African Americans to play professional football since 1933, when football began to distance itself from college football. After the game, professional football accepted people of all skin color on the field. At just 6 feet, 2 inches, 213 pounds, Willis was small for his position but incredibly fast. He was an important part of the four-time AAFC-Champion Browns. Following the AAFC-NFL merger, Willis was a three-time All-Pro in four NFL seasons.

Position Defensive Lineman
Seasons 8 (1946–1953)
Born October 5, 1921, in Columbus, Ohio

Bernie Kosar

F ollowing a successful college career in which he led the Miami Hurricanes to their first national championship, Bernie Kosar entered the NFL Draft with one condition. He wanted to play for his hometown Cleveland Browns. Kosar's stubborn refusal to play anywhere else made him an enemy to some, but it made him a hero in Ohio. Between 1986 and 1991, Kosar was one of the league's top quarterbacks, passing for more than 3,000 yards four times and leading the Browns to three AFC Championship Games. His finest season came in 1987, when he threw for 3,033 yards and 22 touchdowns in just 12 games.

Position Quarterback
Seasons 12 (1985–1996)
Born November 25, 1963, in Youngstown, Ohio

Today's Browns team is made up of many young, talented players who have proven that they are among the best players in the league.

Jordan Cameron

A talented basketball and football player, Jordan Cameron took some time to make up his mind which sport to focus on in college. Cameron decided to stick with football. After spending two seasons with the University of Southern California Trojans as a wide receiver, he switched to tight end for his senior season. The move paid off. In his first two seasons with the Browns, Cameron showed glimpses of the offensive threat he would become, catching 26 passes for 259 yards. In 2013, he exploded for 63 receptions in the team's first 12 games, becoming a key offensive player.

Position Tight End
Seasons 3 (2011–2013)
Born August 8, 1988, in Los Angeles, California

Josh Gordon

It is safe to say that when the Cleveland Browns signed Josh Gordon in the second round of the 2012 Supplemental Draft, they did not know quite what they were getting. Disciplinary issues had prevented Gordon from having much of a college career. However, upon arriving in Cleveland, Gordon applied himself and had an outstanding rookie season, catching 50 receptions for 805 yards. In 2013, Josh Gordon became a superstar. In weeks 12 and 13, he became the first wide receiver in NFL history to record back-to-back 200-yard receiving games. Through the team's first 12 games, Gordon averaged an NFL-best 124.9 receiving yards per game.

Position Wide Receiver
Seasons 2 (2012–2013)
Born April 13, 1991, in Houston, Texas

Joe Thomas

On December 26, 2012, Joe Thomas was selected to participate in his sixth straight Pro Bowl. The selection moved him into elite company with Cleveland legend Jim Brown and 14 other NFL standouts as the only men to accomplish the feat in their first six seasons.

A humble superstar who chose to go fishing with his dad on draft day in 2007, Thomas is the **centerpiece** of the Browns offensive line. In his first six seasons, the 6 feet, 7 inch, 310-pound offensive tackle allowed fewer than 4.5 **sacks** per season.

Position Offensive Tackle
Seasons 7 (2007–2013)
Born December 4, 1984, in Brookfield, Wisconsin

Barkevious Mingo

In the 2013, the Cleveland Browns selected Barkevious Mingo with the sixth overall pick in the NFL Draft. In three years as a defensive end at Louisiana State University, Mingo used his size, speed, and strength to irritate offenses. Today, he uses the same skill set from a different position. Owing to his great speed, the Browns moved Mingo to the outside linebacker position. The team intended on bringing him along slowly. However, when a fast start made Mingo the team leader in sacks, the Browns began to expect more from their 23-year-old rookie.

Position Outside Linebacker
Seasons 1 (2013)
Born October 4, 1990, in Belle Glade, Florida

All-Time Records

62 Career Sacks

Legendary linebacker Clay Matthews, father to NFL players Casey and Clay Matthews, had 62 career sacks in 16 seasons with the Browns.

1,646 Single-season Receiving Yards

In just his second full season, Josh Gordon shattered the Browns previous single-season reception mark of 1,289 yards set by Braylon Edwards.

158
Career Coaching Wins

The Browns were named after Coach Paul Brown, who coached the Browns for the first 17 years of the team's existence. During that time, he racked up 158 wins and seven league championships.

4,132
Single-season Passing Yards

Brian Sipe quarterbacked the Browns' offense from 1974 to 1983. His best season came in 1980, when he passed for 4,132 yards, 30 touchdowns, and was named league MVP.

12,312
All-time Rushing Yards

It took Jim Brown just nine seasons to set a then-NFL record of 12,312 yards. This number still stands as the Browns' all-time rushing record.

Timeline

Throughout the team's history, the Cleveland Browns have had many memorable events that have become defining moments for the team and its fans.

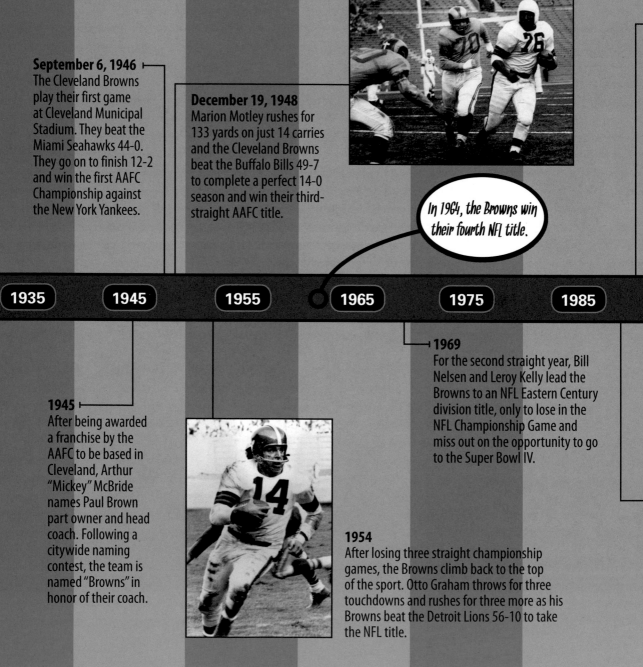

September 6, 1946
The Cleveland Browns play their first game at Cleveland Municipal Stadium. They beat the Miami Seahawks 44-0. They go on to finish 12-2 and win the first AAFC Championship against the New York Yankees.

December 19, 1948
Marion Motley rushes for 133 yards on just 14 carries and the Cleveland Browns beat the Buffalo Bills 49-7 to complete a perfect 14-0 season and win their third-straight AAFC title.

In 1964, the Browns win their fourth NFL title.

| 1935 | 1945 | 1955 | 1965 | 1975 | 1985 |

1969
For the second straight year, Bill Nelsen and Leroy Kelly lead the Browns to an NFL Eastern Century division title, only to lose in the NFL Championship Game and miss out on the opportunity to go to the Super Bowl IV.

1945
After being awarded a franchise by the AAFC to be based in Cleveland, Arthur "Mickey" McBride names Paul Brown part owner and head coach. Following a citywide naming contest, the team is named "Browns" in honor of their coach.

1954
After losing three straight championship games, the Browns climb back to the top of the sport. Otto Graham throws for three touchdowns and rushes for three more as his Browns beat the Detroit Lions 56-10 to take the NFL title.

1987
Bernie Kosar, Kevin Mack, and Webster Slaughter lead a potent offense while Clay Matthews, Frank Minnifield, Hanford Dixon, and Bob Golic make up one of NFL's top defenses. However, the Browns fumble away an opportunity in the AFC Championship Game and fall again to Denver.

CLEVELAND BROWNS

The Future
With young stars like Gordon, Thomas, and Cameron, the Browns' offense has a solid foundation for years to come. However, a few star athletes are unlikely to be enough to end the Browns' playoff drought of nearly 20 years. The Browns will need leadership at the quarterback position and a stellar defense if they hope to win the highly competitive AFC North Division.

In 1999, the Browns play their first game in Cleveland Browns Stadium, later called FirstEnergy Stadium.

| 1990 | 1995 | 2000 | 2005 | 2010 | 2015 |

Art Modell announces his plan to move the Browns to Baltimore at the end of the season. The city of Cleveland sues Modell and wins the rights to the team's name and history.

1986
Coach of the Year Marty Schottenheimer and hometown hero Bernie Kosar lead the Browns to their first playoff win since 1969. In the AFC Championship Game, the Browns have a late lead, but Denver's John Elway leads a 98-yard-touchdown drive and the Browns fall in overtime.

2014
Following years of struggle, new Browns owner Jimmy Haslam hires Mike Pettine to be the team's eighth head coach since 1999. Josh Gordon, Joe Thomas, and Jordan Cameron highlight the current squad.

Write a Biography

Life Story

A person's life story can be the subject of a book. This kind of book is called a biography. Biographies often describe the lives of people who have achieved great success. These people may be alive today, or they may have lived many years ago. Reading a biography can help you learn more about a great person.

Get the Facts

Use this book, and research in the library and on the Internet, to find out more about your favorite Brown. Learn as much about this player as you can. What position does he play? What are his statistics in important categories? Has he set any records? Also, be sure to write down key events in the person's life. What was his childhood like? What has he accomplished off the field? Is there anything else that makes this person special or unusual?

Use the Concept Web

A concept web is a useful research tool. Read the questions in the concept web on the following page. Answer the questions in your notebook. Your answers will help you write a biography.

Concept Web

□

Adulthood
- Where does this individual currently reside?
- Does he or she have a family?

□

Your Opinion
- What did you learn from the books you read in your research?
- Would you suggest these books to others?
- Was anything missing from these books?

□

Childhood
- Where and when was this person born?
- Describe his or her parents, siblings, and friends.
- Did this person grow up in unusual circumstances?

□

Accomplishments off the Field
- What is this person's life's work?
- Has he or she received awards or recognition for accomplishments?
- How have this person's accomplishments served others?

Write a Biography

□

Help and Obstacles
- Did this individual have a positive attitude?
- Did he or she receive help from others?
- Did this person have a mentor?
- Did this person face any hardships?
- If so, how were the hardships overcome?

□

Accomplishments on the Field
- What records does this person hold?
- What key games and plays have defined his or her career?
- What are his or her stats in categories important to his or her position?

□

Work and Preparation
- What was this person's education?
- What was his or her work experience?
- How does this person work; what is the process he or she uses?

Trivia Time

Take this quiz to test your knowledge of the Cleveland Browns.
The answers are printed upside-down under each question.

1 Who were the Cleveland Browns named after?

A. Paul Brown

2 How many Browns are enshrined in the Pro Football Hall of Fame?

A. 16

3 How many AAFC championships did the Browns win during the league's four-year existence?

A. Four

4 Which hometown hero quarterbacked the Browns to back-to-back AFC Championship Games during the 1980s?

A. Bernie Kosar

5 How many NFL Championships did the Browns win under coach Paul Brown?

A. Three

6 Who holds the Browns' all-time rushing yards record with 12,312 yards?

A. Jim Brown

7 Which defensive standout did the Browns select in the first round of the 2013 NFL Draft?

A. Barkevious Mingo

8 How many MVP awards did Jim Brown receive during his nine-year career?

A. Four

9 What is the color of the Browns' helmets?

A. Burnt orange

10 What is the name given to those in the bleacher seats at FirstEnergy Stadium?

A. Dawg Pound

Key Words

All American Football Conference (AAFC): the AAFC was a professional American football league that challenged the established National Football League from 1946 to 1949.

All-Pro: an NFL player judged to be the best in his position for a given season

backfield: the area of play behind either the offensive or defensive line

centerpiece: a player intended to be the focus of attention

color barrier: an unspoken social code of racial segregation or discrimination, especially in sports, education, public service, and the like.

draw play: A football play in which the quarterback moves back as if to pass and then hands the ball to the fullback who is running toward the line of scrimmage.

general manager: the team executive responsible for acquiring the rights to player personnel, negotiating their contracts, and reassigning or dismissing players no longer desired on the team

hall of famer: a player judged to be outstanding in a sport

logo: a symbol that stands for a team or organization

merger: a combination of two leagues or teams into one

Most Valuable Player (MVP): the player judged to be most valuable to his team's success

National Championships: top achievements for any sport or contest in a particular nation

offensive coordinator: a coaching staff member of a gridiron football team who is in charge of the offense

Pro Bowls: annual all star games for NFL players pitting the best players in the National Football Conference against the best players in the American Football Conference

sacks: when the quarterback, or another offensive player acting as a passer, is tackled behind the line of scrimmage before he can throw a forward pass

Super Bowl: the NFL's annual championship game between the winning team from the NFC and the winning team from the AFC

turf: grass and the surface layer of earth held together by its roots

yards from scrimmage: the total of rushing yards and receiving yards from the yard-line on the field from which the play starts

Index

Log on to www.av2books.com

AV² by Weigl brings you media enhanced books that support active learning. Go to www.av2books.com, and enter the special code found on page 2 of this book. You will gain access to enriched and enhanced content that supplements and complements this book. Content includes video, audio, weblinks, quizzes, a slide show, and activities.

AV² Online Navigation

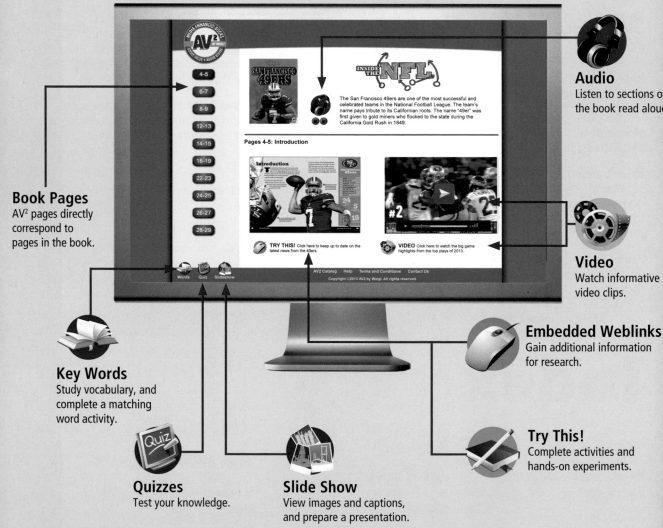

Audio
Listen to sections o
the book read alou

Video
Watch informative
video clips.

Book Pages
AV² pages directly
correspond to
pages in the book.

Embedded Weblinks
Gain additional information
for research.

Key Words
Study vocabulary, and
complete a matching
word activity.

Try This!
Complete activities and
hands-on experiments.

Quizzes
Test your knowledge.

Slide Show
View images and captions,
and prepare a presentation.

AV² was built to bridge the gap between print and digital. We encourage you to tell us what you like and what you want to see in the future.

Sign up to be an AV² Ambassador at www.av2books.com/ambassador.